CW00531486

DRAGON'S WORLD

Dragon's World Ltd
Limpsfield
Surrey RH8 0DY
Great Britain

First published by Dragon's World Ltd 1994

The catalogue record for this book is available from the British Library

ISBN 1 85028 289 7

TEXT compiled by Jeanne Griffiths
EDITOR: Daniel Giles
ART DIRECTOR: John Strange
EDITORIAL DIRECTOR: Pippa Rubinstein

Printed in Hong Kong

Ducks

DRAGON'S WORLD

❈ NATURE'S TREASURES ❈

Shelduck
Tadorna tadorna

The Shelduck's moult migration is one of the strangest phenomena in the bird world. Ducklings stay in 'creches', where they are tended by a few mature birds. The rest of the adults fly hundreds of miles to places like the Elbe estuary, where each October they shed their flight feathers.

> *Ducks require no ship or sail*
> *Bellied on the foamy skies,*
> *Who scud north. Male and female*
> *Make a slight nest to arise*
> *Where they overtake the spring,*
> *Which clogs with muddy going.*

JOHN CROWE RANSOM
WHAT DUCKS REQUIRE

European Wigeon
Anas penelope

The dramatic sight of a huge flock of Wigeon flying to feed on marshes on a winter's evening, is enhanced by the strange whistling calls which keep the birds together. Wigeon are grazers, cropping fields and marshes by night, and sleeping by day.

Time cannot break the bird's wing
  from the bird.
Bird and wing together
Go down, one feather

EDNA ST VINCENT MILLAY
TO A YOUNG POET

American Wigeon
Anas americana

Often called Baldpate, due to the white crown of the male, the American Wigeon makes long migrations. Although usually tolerant of other Wigeon, most pairs prefer their own pond. Like other ground-nesting duck, the female covers her eggs when she goes to feed.

> *Four duck on a pond,*
> *A grass-bank beyond,*
> *A blue sky of spring,*
> *White clouds on the wing*

WILLIAM ALLINGHAM
A MEMORY

Gadwall
Anas strepera

Gadwells prefer still, shallow marshes,
which they often share with gulls and
terns. They do not appear to have adapted
to other habitats as these marshes have
been drained. Females often return to their
place of origin to breed, taking their
current mates with them.

> *Glory be to God for dappled things -*
> *For skies of couple-colour as a*
> *   brinded cow;*
> *For rose-moles all in stipple upon*
> *   trout that swim*

GERARD MANLEY HOPKINS
PIED BEAUTY

Teal,
or Green-winged Teal
Anas crecca

The most common of all the northern duck, Teal breed in the forest regions of the Northern Hemisphere, forming a ring around the Pole. They often travel over 1,500 kilometres to reach moulting grounds further south.

Fill the lake with wild-fowl;
Fill the marsh with snipe;
While on dreary moorlands
Lonely curlew pipe.

CHARLES KINGSLEY
ODE TO THE NORTH-EAST WIND

Mallard
Anas platyrhynchos

The Mallard is the world's most familiar
duck. It feeds both in water and on land.
The female builds her nest in vegetation,
under boulders, and even in tree holes,
which she lines with quantities of down.

*A mallard, wing-stretched in the
sun,*
*Watching from the back of a beer-
bubble stream*
Her ducklings, one after one,
Daring, dipping in dazzling weed,
Nuzzling joyful mud.

PHOEBE HESKETH
THE MALLARD

Black Duck
Anas rubripes

The North American Black Duck is a surface feeder, dabbling and up-ending to find food. Unlike other ducks, male and female form partnerships that may last for years, separating only during the moult period and re-establishing their bond once they can both fly again.

> *All along the backwater,*
> *Through the rushes tall,*
> *Ducks are a-dabbling*
> *Up tails all!*

KENNETH GRAHAME
THE WIND IN THE WILLOWS

Pintail
Anas acuta

Also known as Sea Pheasant, the elegant Pintail spends much of its time up-ending in search of food. Unusually for duck, the male is often present during the incubation of the eggs, and may even accompany the female as she leads her newly hatched brood to the water.

> *By the Lake's margin I mark'd her lie —*
> *The wide, weird lake where alders sigh —*
> *A fair young thing with a shy, soft eye*

CHARLES STUART CALVERLEY
SHELTER

Garganey
Anas querquedula

Although most ducks are migrants,
Garganey make exceptionally long
journeys, often flying non-stop over the
Mediterranean and the Sahara on their
way to southern India, South East Asia and
Africa. They use a loop migration, always
returning by a different route.

The bees forget to sip their honey;
  drunken with light
  they foolishly hover and hum.
The ducks in the islands of the river
  clamour in joy for mere nothing.

SIR RABINDRANATH TAGORE
THE GARDENER

Northern Shoveler
Anas clypeata

The most obvious feature of this long-distance migrant is its spoon-shaped bill, which it uses to sieve out tiny particles of food from surface water. The Northern Shoveler also dives for food.

And soon that toil shall end;
Soon shalt thou find a summer
*   home, and rest,*
And scream among thy fellows; reed
*   shall bend,*
Soon, o'er thy sheltered nest.

WILLIAM CULLEN BRYANT
TO A WATERFOWL

Red-crested Pochard
Netta rufina

This attractive duck is widely kept in
captivity. Females frequently lay their eggs
in the nests of other ducks. Up to thirty-
nine eggs have been found in one nest
alone. Inspite of this, about half the eggs
laid produce fledged young – a higher
proportion than many other duck.

> *But Nature, graciously inclined*
> *With liberal hand to please us*
> *Has to her boundless beauty joined*
> *A boundless bent to ease us.*

GEORGE GRANVILLE
CLOE

Pochard
Aythya ferina

Pochard make long migratory flights from winter to summer feeding grounds. They also perform moult migrations which can involve over 50,000 birds flocking to a particular reservoir or lake. Like other duck, Pochards conserve energy on long journeys by flying in 'V' formation. Each member gets extra lift from the slip-stream of the bird in front.

From the troubles of the world
I turn to ducks,
Beautiful comical things

FREDERICK HARVEY WILLIAMS
DUCKS

Ferruginous Duck
Aythya nyroca

Found in shallow fresh waters rich in vegetation, this elusive creature can search under water for food for up to fifty seconds. Unlike many species of diving duck, it rarely forms large flocks and is usually found in parties of four or six.

O souls not understood,
What a wild cry in the pool;
What things have farm ducks seen
That they cry so — huddle and cry?

JOHN MASEFIELD
THE WILD DUCK

Tufted Duck
Aythya fuligula

Since it was first identified in Iceland in 1895, the Tufted Duck has become common across the Northern Hemisphere, taking advantage of man-made waters. Flocks of 2,000 or more can often be seen on reservoirs.

> *The sun descending in the west,*
> *The evening star does shine;*
> *The birds are silent in their nest,*
> *And I must seek for mine.*

WILLIAM BLAKE
NIGHT

Greater Scaup
Aythya marila

Greater Scaup can migrate over 4,000 kilometres from breeding grounds in the north to the milder coasts of the east and west, where they pass the winter. They particularly like to gather around distillery outfalls, where grain waste enters the sea.

> *Behold the duck,*
> *It does not cluck,*
> *A cluck it lacks,*
> *It quacks.*
> *It is especially fond*
> *Of a puddle or a pond.*

OGDEN NASH
THE DUCK

King Eider
Somateria spectabilis

King Eider inhabit some of the world's most hostile environments. They breed in the northern most tundra of the Arctic Circle, and winter at the edge of the pack ice. Breeding lasts just sixty days.

> *What would the world be, once bereft*
> *Of wet and of wilderness? Let them be left,*
> *O Let them be left, wildness and wet;*
> *Long live the weeds and the wilderness yet.*

GERARD MANLEY HOPKINS
INVERSNAID

Long-tailed Duck
Clangula hyemalis

Long-tails, or Old Squaw, can dive to
depths of thiry-five metres. Like most
other duck, the male and female plumage
differs, but Long-tails are unusual in
having equally distinctive summer and
winter plumages.

The cloud shadows of midnight
possess their own repose,
For the weary winds are silent, or
the moon is in the deep:
Some respite to its turbulence
unresting ocean knows

PERCY BYSSHE SHELLEY
STANZSAS

Common Goldeneye
Bucephala clangula

Goldeneye males have an elaborate series of displays. In the 'kick display', the male stretches his head and neck forward before throwing his head back until it rests on his body with bill pointing sky-wards, while simultaneously kicking backwards with his feet.

> *Happy being! Equally fitted for travelling through the air and the water, and not altogether denied the pleasure of walking on the shore…*
>
> JOHN JAMES AUDUBON
> **NOTES FROM HIS JOURNAL, 1820**

Red-breasted Merganser
Mergus serrator

Mergansers are fish-eaters, whose thin, serrated bills have teeth-like protrusions to grip slippery prey. Unlike other diving duck, they use both feet and wings for high-speed underwater swimming. Small fish are swallowed below the water, while larger ones are brought to the surface.

In what lies the fascination of ducks? For an overwhelming fascination it is, and one that grows and becomes more and more commanding.

PHYLLIS BARCLAY-SMITH
A BOOK OF DUCKS

Ruddy Duck

Oxyura jamaicensis

The Ruddy Duck is a member of the
stifftail group and a native of the New
World, although it has been introduced
into Europe. Its broad spatulate bill allows
it to sieve out food from the mud.
Remarkably, the Ruddy Duck can sink
below the surface without diving,
although it finds flying difficult. Take-off
requires much frantic beating of its wings.

If nature smiles – the Mother must
I'm sure, at many a whim
Of Her eccentric family –
Is She so much to blame?

EMILY DICKINSON
COMPLETE POEMS, No 1085

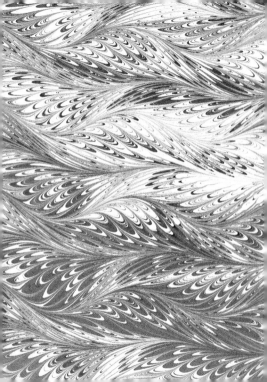